ADVOCACY

Establishment of Rights
Training and Reference Manual

Doc Dengenis
Bargaining Consultant

Wildcat–Lava Bear Publications

January 2020

Third Printing

DEDICATION

This book is dedicated to my mother, Rosamond Dengenis, and my brothers, Frank Joseph Dengenis, Jr., and Michael Dengenis; all deceased. In addition, it is for my beloved children, Petra Dengenis Roberts, Rhyne Champ Dengenis, Brig Dengenis; my first grandson, Burton Roberts; and son-in-law, Ryan Roberts.

Also Advocacy Establishment of Rights is for the Hartford Brothers: Bob Raffalo, Tom Sonnone, George Kilray, and Michael John Stelman. Finally, the book is to memorialize the life and times of The Old Fat City Athletic Club from Bend, Oregon: Gary Olson, Oran Teator, Michael E. Carter, Eldon Pearson, and Dennis "Goose" Gasbar—when life was simple but great fun, especially "The Spring Fling and The Sno-Ball."

TABLE OF CONTENTS

Generic Management Team Packet
THE ACCUSED — ROLE PLAY

Generic Association Team Packet
THE ACCUSED — ROLE PLAY

PREFACE

Advocacy Establishment of Rights explains the important foundations of basic advocacy. This is a valuable resource document for all advocate trainees and trainers, regardless of skill level or experience.

Readers will have the opportunity to develop and practice advocacy skills, techniques, tactics, and strategies in a wide variety of thirty-five exercises, cases, problems, scenarios, and a final advocacy role-play simulation. The emphasis is on developing advocacy skills, exploring rights to representation, Duty of Fair Representation, due process safeguards, questioning strategies, verbal skills, Just Cause, Weingarten Rules, insubordination, Association Code of Conduct, grievance adjudication, and learning about guidelines for administrative meetings. A comprehensive analysis of Past Practice concepts is covered in great detail.

This Advocacy book is a result of thirty years of successful advocacy, grievance adjudication, arbitration, organizing, and training experiences. These concepts are explored in depth empowering the reader with new tools to deal with local advocacy problems.

LIFE

Life as a consultant and author without regular eight-to-five responsibilities is great; I celebrate the successful completion and publishing of my second book, *Advocacy Establishment of Rights*.

The experience was fun and professionally fulfilling. My motivation was to leave some of the knowledge I acquired during my career to the next generation of advocate leaders, both staff and governance.

ACKNOWLEDGMENTS

Brig Dengenis provided computer expertise and advice pertinent to the successful completion of *Advocacy Establishment of Rights*. Rebecca Tait provided valuable copy editing and proofreading services. Odis Avritt was responsible for the photo on the back cover. The front and back covers were created and designed by Brig Dengenis.

FACILITIES LIST

1. One big training room with sufficient tables for a maximum of four trainees per table (one team per table).

2. One flip chart

Also:

1. Name tags

2. Large felt-tip pens

3. Tape

4. Parking Lot sheet(s)

5. Certificates

6. Rewards

PREFERABLE ROOM ARRANGEMENT
(Tables in chevron style)

Flipchart	Podium	Staff Table
X	X X	X X
X X	X X	X X
X X	X	X
X	X X	X X
X X	X X	X X
X X	X	X
X	X X	X X
X X	X X	X X
X X	X	X

PARKING LOT

THREE BONES OF LIFE

1) The first bone is the funny bone.
   + Always have a sense of humor and experience a good "belly laugh" every day.

2) The second bone is the wishbone.
   + Think big with lofty goals so your ideas will grow and hitch your dreams to a high star.

3) The third important bone is the backbone.
   + The "Advocacy Bone" gives you the grit, fortitude, courage, and desire to make your dreams come true.

TEAM BUILDING

Respond individually to each question, one question at a time.

1. My name is _____.

2. I have worked in the _____ for the last _____ years.

3. I was born in the city of _____, state of

    _____.

4. My early childhood years were in the city of _____,

    state of _____.

5. My favorite television program while I was in high school was

    _____.

6. My main responsibilities at work are

    _____

    _____.

7. The sum total of my Advocacy experience is

    _____

    _____.

EXPECTATION SHARING

Complete the sentence stems in any way you so choose.

If by the end of this training I…

_____

_____

_____

_____

_____

_____

_____

then the advocacy training was a success.

WORKPLACE FACTS OF LIFE

1. There are natural conflicts inherent in the employee-employer relationship because of the difference between employee and employer values.

2. Natural conflicts will occur whether a traditional or collaborative culture exists in the employment relationship. The employer has the most power and employees must operate as individuals in a non-union workplace.

3. The employees must be able to act collectively in order to create a balance of power to effectively manage these conflicts and to eliminate injustices and sub-standard pay and working conditions.

4. The ability to survive and thrive in managing workplace conflict by collective action is essential in order to be successful in Association advocacy; otherwise employees will lose power.

"AN INJURY TO ONE IS AN INJURY TO ALL."

➢ Means that the mistreatment of any individual employee creates the possibility of mistreatment for *every* employee.

➢ *Requires* workers come to the support and defense of fellow workers who are threatened.

➢ Creates a *balance of power* between the employer and the employees, and

➢ is the foundation of *solidarity* among employees.

This is the basic premise of unionism.

BEHAVIORS THAT PROMOTE/UNDERMINE SOLIDARITY

+

Promoting Behaviors

- Seek the common/collective good.
- Communicate with colleagues when problems arise.
- Support, defend, and advocate for colleagues.
- Act collectively.
- Your primary interest is for benefit of colleagues.

—

Undermining Behaviors

- Act solely in your own self-interest.
- Go first to Management when problems arise.
- Criticize colleagues to other employees.
- Make individual decisions and ignore others.
- Your primary main interests are for Management.

AN ADVOCATE

A

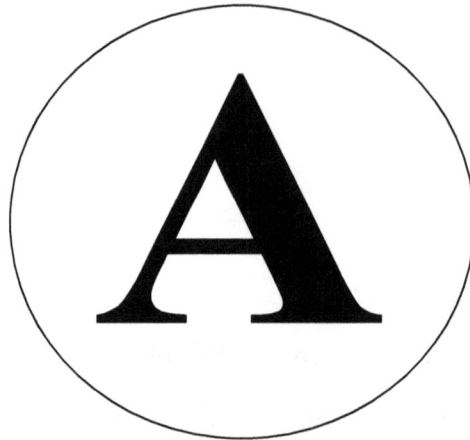

"...ONE SUMMONED TO AID
...WHO PLEADS THE CAUSE
...AN UPHOLDER: A DEFENDER."
— Webster

WHAT IT MEANS TO BE AN ADVOCATE

Webster defines an advocate as:

One that pleads the cause of another;

One who defends or maintains a cause or proposal.

As an Association Advocate, you will:

❖ Seek out employees who have concerns about issues.

❖ Respect the employee's position and point of view.

❖ Offer encouragement, support, understanding and acknowledgement of the problem or issue.

❖ Defend rights and not prejudge the employee.

❖ Strictly observe the employee's right to confidentiality.

❖ Thoroughly investigate the problem or issue.

❖ If the problem is serious, contact your professional staff person and/or attorney immediately.

ADVOCACY

ADVOCACY is the glue that holds us together.

ADVOCACY is how we survive in this or any society. German pastor and anti-Nazi activist, Martin Niemoller, said it best:

> *First they came for the Jews and I did not speak out—because I was not a Jew.*
>
> *Then they came for the communists and I did not speak out—because I was not a communist.*
>
> *Then they came for the trade unionists and I did not speak out—because I was not a trade unionist.*
>
> *Then they came for the Catholics, and I did not speak out—because I was a Protestant.*
>
> *Then they came for me—and by then no one was left to speak out for me.*

ADVOCACY EXERCISE 1

Circle the words appropriate for Advocacy as an Association Representative.

1. Encouragement

2. Due Process

3. Defend

4. Accommodate

5. Appease

6. Judge

7. Confidential

8. Apathy

9. Soft

10. Investigate

11. Surrender

12. Support

13. Protect

ADVOCACY EXERCISE 1 ANSWERS

Circle the words appropriate for Advocacy as an Association Representative.

1.	**Encouragement**	☆
2.	**Due Process**	☆
3.	**Defend**	☆

4. Accommodate

5. Appease

6. Judge

7.	**Confidential**	☆

8. Apathy

9. Soft

10.	**Investigate**	☆

11. Surrender

12.	**Support**	☆
13.	**Protect**	☆

ASSOCIATION ADVOCATE'S MAIN RESPONSIBILITY
EXERCISE 2

This is an exercise in the general objectives or goals of the Association Advocate's job. Listed below are four different objectives or goals that might serve as a guide for Association Advocates. *For the purpose of this exercise, you are required to choose only one of the four listed statements, even if no single one satisfies you entirely; each choice has drawbacks.* Analyze and select the most acceptable answer. Most importantly, be ready to explain and defend your choice.

1.   The Association Advocate's responsibility is to promote harmony between Management and the employees. If you succeed in this objective, good Labor-Management relations exist and everyone is satisfied. Filing grievances is a last resort and a valid way of resolving problems to meet the needs of members who want to enforce the contract.

2.   The Association Advocate's responsibility is to ensure all members abide by the rules, regulations, and provisions related to and in the contract. The rules are for the mutual benefit of Management and employees. If everyone abides by them there will not be any serious problems, and as a consequence, "Peace in the Valley."

3.   The Association Advocate's responsibility is to be the employee's advocate and defender, handling the employee's problems, grievances, and complaints without prejudging right or wrong, good or bad.

4.   The Association Advocate's responsibility is to be a peacemaker between the employees and Management and also among the employees. Many problems arise because of conflicts between employees, and an effective Advocate resolves these types of problems as well as the conflicts between employees and Management.

ASSOCIATION ADVOCATE'S MAIN RESPONSIBILITY
EXERCISE 2 DISCUSSION

In light of the information just covered, consider what might occur if any of these four options were implemented.

OPTION #1 may lead members to conclude that harmony with Management is more important than their rights and/or needs with a message of "Peace in the Valley." While good working relations are important, it is best achieved through mutual respect and enforcement of contract rights. The aggressive pursuit of valid grievances does not demonstrate a lack of harmony; rather, the Association is working to satisfy the needs of members who believe they have enforceable rights. The grievance procedure is a constructive way to solve problems.

OPTION #2 makes the Association the disciplinarian for Management. It is Management's role to ensure everyone lives up to the contract. The Association role is to ensure Management does not violate the contract while enforcing rules. In this case members will eventually lose trust in the Association.

OPTION #3 requires the Associate Advocate to support positions that may not be in the best interest of the Association. However, if the Association continually processes grievances without merit, the grievance process is trivialized and meritorious grievances become much harder to process.

OPTION #4 has many of the same drawbacks as Option #1. In addition, under this choice the Association is given the responsibility of standing between member's disagreements. If a conflict between members can be solved by the advocate addressing the root of the conflict in terms of the employer/employee relationship, great; otherwise the Association may be looked upon as the enemy if one member is perceived as the "winner" and the other member as the "loser."

ADVOCATE'S RESPONSIBILITY SCENARIO 3
ALL TRAINEES

Management has exceeded the budget for employee development and training because one group of employees used all funds allocated in the Agreement to implement a program started on a government grant. The Association was instrumental in securing the grant and advocated the need for training since this new innovative program would save and create new jobs in the long run. A second group of employees is complaining about lack of access to training funds.

Management's position is the Association advocated for the grant so they expect the Association to resolve this problem.

The following provision is in the Agreement: Release time for Employee Development and Training. Employees may be released from duties in order to attend employee development and training. The use of paid released time shall be, to the extent possible, equally distributed to all employees within departments.

1. Using options 1–4 of "The Most Important Part of an Association Advocate's Main Responsibility," what is the role of the representative in this case?

2. What should the Association do?

3. Develop a strategy.

RIGHTS TO REPRESENTATION

1. All Association bargaining unit members have the right to representation in any alleged violation of the contract.

2. The role of an employee organization is to fairly represent members and defend their due process and other contractual and legal rights.

3. The role of the Association is to listen to the complaint of a member, devise the best resolution strategy, and achieve it the best way possible.

4. "The Rule of the Greater Good" means the Association can refuse to file a grievance if winning would adversely affect either segments of or the entire bargaining unit.

5. Employees have the right to self-organization; to form, join, or assist labor organizations; to bargain collectively through representatives of their own choosing; and to engage in other concerted activities for the purpose of collective bargaining or other mutual aid or protection.

REPRESENTATION CASE 4
ALL TRAINEES

A twenty-year employee with a clean record was given a ticket for drunk driving. The member claimed he was innocent because the police were "out to get him" since he was a high-profile citizen. He pleaded not guilty to the driving charge and a jury trial was scheduled the next month. He said he gargled with Listerine® before leaving home, and, as a result, the policewoman mistakenly believed she smelled alcohol on his breath. Also, he had an inner ear infection that caused him to stumble, at times, when he walked. Part of his job was handling hazardous materials. The contract has a standard Just Cause clause.

Management fired him for the driving charge. The member and his Advocate scheduled a meeting with Management to dispute the firing.

Prepare arguments for the Management meeting.

REPRESENTATION CASE 5
K–12 EDUCATORS AND CLASSIFIED

Michelle Mistake calls you and says a fourth grade special education student punched her in the face. In a defensive reaction, Michelle raised her hand to defend herself from a second blow and the student's frail arm was broken. She is devastated. The principal has scheduled a fact-finding meeting with her and advised Michelle of her right to representation. She wants to resign because she is a first year teacher. She comes to you for consultation. What do you tell her? She also asks if the Association will provide assistance if she is charged with a felony assault and battery? Ms. Mistake is a halftime paraprofessional and a halftime teacher who pays dues and is a member of both the Teacher and Classified Associations.

Instructions:

1.   Devise a representation strategy for a meeting with the principal.

2.   What would you tell Michelle to do in the future?

DUTY OF FAIR REPRESENTATION (DFR)

A. "The employee organization recognized or certified as the exclusive representative for the purpose of meeting and negotiating shall fairly represent each and every employee in the appropriate unit."

B. Bargaining unit members are entitled by law to the "Duty of Fair Representation" by their organization.

GENERAL DUTY OF FAIR REPRESENTATION

Application of the general Duty of Fair Representation to specific situations has resulted in the development of the following specific duties the Association owes to all unit employees:

1. **Duty** to represent all unit employees.

2. **Duty** to negotiate on behalf of all unit employees and consider non-joiner views concerning negotiations.

3. **Duty** to be familiar with and enforce the contract.

4. **Duty** to advise unit employees of their legal rights in the context of the contract.

5. **Duty** to process grievance in a non-arbitrary, nondiscriminatory and good faith manner.

6. **Duty** to investigate grievances and keep accurate and complete records.

7. **Duty** to satisfy contractual time limits.

8. **Duty** to notify a grievant of Association decisions.

9. **Duty** to present a good arbitration case.

10. **Duty** to allow a grievant to have his/her attorney present at arbitration proceedings.

DFR FREQUENTLY ASKED QUESTIONS

1.   Who can declare breach of the duty?

   *   Bargaining Unit Members only.

2.   What constitutes breach of duty?

   *   If the Association acts in an arbitrary, discriminatory or bad faith manner toward a unit member.

3.   What must be proven for a breach of duty?

   *   The Association did act in an arbitrary, discriminatory or in a bad faith manner.

   *   The Association's conduct was in violation of an obligation it had with the existing labor law.

4.   Who is responsible for the duty?

   *   Association Officers, Association Representatives, and Association Agents.

DUTY OF FAIR REPRESENTATION
QUIZ 6

Indicate whether you agree (A) or disagree (D) with the following statements:

_____ 1. The Association has a duty to represent Representation-Fee Payers (nonmembers)* in contractual matters.

_____ 2. "The Rule of the Greater Good" is the Association can refuse to file any grievance that negatively impacts other unit members.

_____ 3. The Association has complied with the Duty of Fair Representation once a representative refers a contract issue to the President or staff person.

_____ 4. The Association is obligated to provide legal counsel for a Representation-Fee Payer member in a legal hearing.

_____ 5. The Association owns the grievance procedure so it can require all grievances to be processed through its Grievance Committee.

_____ 6. The Association does not have to investigate low-priority grievances.

_____ 7. Contractual timelines are waived when the Association Representative or the Association President is out because of a family illness.

_____ 8. The Association completes its obligation to the grievant once it receives the request from the grievant to proceed to arbitration.

_____ 9. The person presenting an arbitration case must be prepared.

_____ 10. A member may bring his/her own attorney to an arbitration hearing.

_____ 11. Association Representatives have a duty to be familiar with the contract.

_____ 12. The Association has no duty to consider fee-payer (nonmember) views concerning negotiations.

_____ 13. The Human Relations Director can sue the Association for lack of duty to fairly represent on behalf of Fee Payers.

_____ 14. The Association cannot act in a bad faith manner or it could be named in a Duty of Fair Representation charge.

_____ 15. A breach of duty to fairly represent can result because of arbitrary and/or discriminatory Association decisions.

---

*Fee payers are nonmembers who pay a fee to the Association for bargaining, contract maintenance costs, but not for dues used for political purposes.

DUTY OF FAIR REPRESENTATION
QUIZ 6 ANSWERS

Indicate whether you agree (A) or disagree (D) with the following statements.

A 1. The Association has a duty to represent Representation-Fee Payers (nonmembers)* in contractual matters.

A 2. "The Rule of the Greater Good" is the Association can refuse to file any grievance that negatively impacts other unit members.

D 3. The Association has complied with the Duty of Fair Representation once a representative refers a contract issue to the President or staff person.

D 4. The Association is obligated to provide legal counsel for a Representation-Fee Payer member in a legal hearing.

A 5. The Association owns the grievance procedure so it can require all grievances to be processed through its Grievance Committee.

D 6. The Association does not have to investigate low priority grievances.

D 7. Contractual timelines are waived when the Association Representative or the Association President is out because of a family illness.

D 8. The Association completes its obligation to the grievant once it receives the request from the grievant to proceed to arbitration.

A 9. The person presenting an arbitration case must be prepared.

A 10. A member may bring his/her own attorney to an arbitration hearing.

A 11. Association Representatives have a duty to be familiar with the contract.

D 12. The Association has no duty to consider fee-payer (nonmember) views concerning negotiations.

D 13. The Human Relations Director can sue the Association for lack of duty to fairly represent on behalf of fee payers.

A 14. The Association cannot act in a bad faith manner or it could be named in a Duty of Fair Representation charge.

A 15. A breach of duty to fairly represent can result because of arbitrary and/or discriminatory Association decisions.

---

*Fee payers are nonmembers who pay a fee to the Association for bargaining, contract maintenance costs, but not for dues used for political purposes.

ADVOCACY PROBLEM 7
ALL TRAINEES

Assume that you are an advocate in a local Association that is developing procedures for handling grievances.

The procedures being developed are to be incorporated in the proposed comprehensive contract the Association will take to the bargaining table shortly.

The Association is the exclusive representative of the members.

One of the advocates moves that the following clause be included in the proposed procedure:

> *The Association shall not support or provide representation for any individual grievant who is not a member (fee payer) of the Association.*

Discuss the implications of this motion, debate the issues raised, and make your recommendations on the next page.

ADVOCACY PROBLEM 7
EXERCISE SHEET

Strategy recommendation:

Reasons:

What is the training issue we reviewed?

DUE PROCESS AND JUST CAUSE

Due Process is the process of "fairness" requiring an employee to be informed of any offense or violation, if charged, deemed severe enough to cause an official act to be taken and presented so the employee understands the charge and is able to provide a defense.

1. Action – Notice of Warning
   Reaction – Is it clear and understandable? Was Just Cause applied?

2. Action – Remediation
   Reaction – What needs to be accomplished?

3. Action – Progress Monitoring
   Reaction – Has Management assisted in remediation?

4. Action – Official Action
   Reaction – Was it timely? Was contract followed?

KEY WORDS in the PROCESS

1. Reasonable inquiry?
2. Allowed to question accuser?
3. Any discrimination during process?
4. Agreement, laws, and policies followed?
5. Punishment consistent with alleged offense?

DUE PROCESS SAFEGUARDS

Minimum procedural safeguards of due process
(U.S. Supreme Court, Goldberg v. Kelly)

1. The opportunity to be heard at a reasonable time and in a reasonable manner.

2. Timely and adequate notice detailing the reasons for a proposed discipline.

3. An effective opportunity to defend by presenting arguments and evidence orally.

4. An opportunity to confront and cross-examine adverse witnesses.

5. The right to retain an advocate and/or attorney.

6. A decision resting solely on the legal rules and evidence adduced at the time of the hearing.

7. A statement by the decision maker of the reasons for the final decision and the evidence relied on in the case.

8. An impartial final decision maker.

DUE PROCESS SAFEGUARDS
QUIZ 8

+ for True   0 for False

_____1.   An essential element of due process is the right to an impartial decision maker.

_____2.   Due process means the right to retain an advocate and/or attorney unless the case involves sexual harassment against another employee.

_____3.   Management does not have to give timely and adequate notice in a discipline case if the information is confidential.

_____4.   Association advocates must be given an opportunity to cross-examine witnesses.

_____5.   Due process includes being heard at a reasonable time, given timely notice, the opportunity to present arguments, and having the final decision based on legal precedents.

DUE PROCESS SAFEGUARDS
QUIZ 8 ANSWERS

+ for True   0 for False

+   1.   An essential element of due process is the right to an impartial decision maker.

0   2.   Due process means the right to retain an advocate and/or attorney unless the case involves sexual harassment against another employee.

0   3.   Management does not have to give timely and adequate notice in a discipline case if the information is confidential.

+   4.   Association advocates must be given an opportunity to cross-examine witnesses.

+   5.   Due process includes being heard at a reasonable time, given timely notice, the opportunity to present arguments, and having the final decision based on legal precedents.

WHAT DOES JUST CAUSE MEAN?

Standard "Just Cause" Contract Clause

"No employee shall be disciplined, reprimanded, or reduced in compensation without Just Cause."

Seven Key Tests of Just Cause by Arbitrator Carroll R. Daugherty

A "no" answer to one or more of the questions means that <u>Just Cause either was not satisfied or seriously weakened</u> because some arbitrary, capricious, or discriminatory element was present.

1.   NOTICE: Did Management give to the employee forewarning or foreknowledge of the possible or probable consequences of the employee's disciplinary conduct?

2.   REASONABLE RULE OR ORDER: Was Management's rule or managerial order reasonably related to (a) orderly, efficient, and safe operation of the Employer's business, and (b) the performance Management might properly expect of the employee?

3.   INVESTIGATION: Did the Employer, before administering the discipline to an employee, make an effort to discover whether the employee did in fact violate or disobey a rule or order of Management?

4.   FAIR INVESTIGATION: Was Management's investigation conducted fairly and objectively?

5.   PROOF: At the investigation, did the "judge" obtain substantial evidence or proof the employee was guilty as charged.

6.   EQUAL TREATMENT: Has Management applied its rules, orders and penalties even-handedly and without discrimination to all employees?

7.   PENALTY: Was the degree of discipline administered by Management in a particular case reasonably related to (a) the seriousness of the employee's *proven* offense, and (b) the record of the employee in his service with the Employer?

ASSOCIATION JUST CAUSE GUIDELINES

The basic Association questions are:

1.   Was the discipline defensible?

2.   Was the penalty just?

        If the answer is "No" to either 1 or 2 then proceed to—

3.   Was the employee's conduct comparable to what a reasonable and prudent person would have done under the existing circumstances?

4.   Was the employee's conduct in accordance with the customs, practices, standards of justice and fair dealing prevalent in the community and/or industry or workplace?

        A "yes" answer to either 3 or 4 means
        the advocacy moves forward to arbitration.

THREE MAJOR STANDARDS OF JUST CAUSE

1.   The employee was afforded fundamental due process rights.

   a. The employee must have had forewarning and/or foreknowledge the conduct would lead to discipline.

   b. The employee had a fair investigation conducted and the rules were consistently applied and enforced evenly.

2.   Management must prove charges/allegations against employee. The "Burden of Proof" in discipline cases is on Management.

3.   The penalty imposed was reasonably related to the seriousness of the offense(s), the employee's disciplinary record, and any mitigating or extenuating circumstances.

ASSOCIATION JUST CAUSE CORNERSTONES
WHAT THE ASSOCIATION/EMPLOYEE MUST PROVE

1.   The employee's conduct is what a reasonable and prudent person would have done given the existing circumstances.

2.   The employee's conduct was in accordance with the customs, practices, standards of justice and fair dealing prevalent in the community, industry, and/or workplace.

3.   The discipline was either indefensible and/or the penalty was unjust.

JUST CAUSE FINAL EXAM 9: K–12 EDUCATORS

Answering "Yes" means it meets the test of Just Cause and
"No" indicates it does not meet the test of Just Cause.

Circle correct answer "Yes" or "No."

Situations

1. A teacher was five minutes late to work one time, and, as a result, is fired.

    Yes   No

2. A certified teacher, born in France, was observed drinking a glass of wine at noon on school property while at work. She claimed she did not realize there was a rule against drinking wine with her meal because in her culture wine is considered part of the food. She was given a written reprimand.

    Yes   No

3. A teacher discovered her son and three other football players drinking at her home when she returned on a holiday weekend. She reported the incident to her supervisor, the elementary principal, and made the boys turn themselves in to the coach (who does not teach), who failed to inform the superintendent. The superintendent wrote a letter of reprimand to the teacher for failure to report the students to her or to the athletic director. (The position of athletic director was vacant at the time.) The district policy contained no reporting procedure.

    Yes   No

Discussion – What reporting responsibilities do employees have in these cases? What responsibilities does the district have to inform employees of these reporting policies if they do exist?

4. A driver education teacher was ticketed for drunk driving while on vacation in another state. The teacher claimed he was innocent and will face a jury trial sometime in the near future. The district suspended him without pay.

    Yes   No

5. A teacher was accused of molesting students. After district officials interviewed several students, he was suspended with pay pending a trial date. He claimed he should have received an oral warning as the first step in a discipline, not suspended.

    Yes   No

6. An employee was convicted of running an illegal bookmaking operation from her house. The district fired her. She contacted the Association and wanted to file a grievance because there was no specific written rule or policy against this type of activity.

    Yes   No

7. An employee was ordered by the principal to search students on the playground after a telephone call alerted the district a student had a small homemade pipe bomb. The teacher refused. The principal wrote a letter of reprimand for failure to comply with an order. She filed a grievance.

    Yes   No

8. A teacher failed to file his weekly lesson plan with the principal. It was his first offense. The principal suspended him without pay for three days.

    Yes   No

JUST CAUSE FINAL EXAM 9 ANSWERS: K–12 EDUCATORS

Answering "Yes" means it meets the test of Just Cause and
"No" indicates it does not meet the test of Just Cause.

Circle correct answer "Yes" or "No."

Situations

1. A teacher was five minutes late to work one time, and, as a result, is fired.

   Yes **No**

2. A certified teacher, born in France, was observed drinking a glass of wine at noon on school property while at work. She claimed she did not realize there was a rule against drinking wine with her meal because in her culture wine is considered part of the food. She was given a written reprimand.

   Yes No

3. A teacher discovered her son and three other football players drinking at her home when she returned on a holiday weekend. She reported the incident to her supervisor, the elementary principal, and made the boys turn themselves in to the coach (who does not teach), who failed to inform the superintendent. The superintendent wrote a letter of reprimand to the teacher for failure to report the students to her or to the athletic director. (The position of athletic director was vacant at the time.) The district policy contained no reporting procedure.

   Yes **No**

Discussion – What reporting responsibilities do employees have in these cases? What responsibilities does the district have to inform employees of these reporting policies if they do exist?

4. A driver education teacher was ticketed for drunk driving while on vacation in another state. The teacher claimed he was innocent and will face a jury trial sometime in the near future. The district suspended him without pay.

   Yes **No**

5. A teacher was accused of molesting students. After district officials interviewed several students, he was suspended with pay pending a trial date. He claimed he should have received an oral warning as the first step in a discipline, not suspended.

   Yes No

6. An employee was convicted of running an illegal bookmaking operation from her house. The district fired her. She contacted the Association and wanted to file a grievance because there was no specific written rule or policy against this type of activity.

   Yes No

7. An employee was ordered by the principal to search students on the playground after a telephone call alerted the district a student had a small homemade pipe bomb. The teacher refused. The principal wrote a letter of reprimand for failure to comply with an order. She filed a grievance.

   Yes **No**

8. A teacher failed to file his weekly lesson plan with the principal. It was his first offense. The principal suspended him without pay for three days.

   Yes **No**

JUST CAUSE FINAL EXAM 10
FACULTY AND ALL CLASSIFIED

Answering "Yes" means it meets the standards and guidelines of Just Cause
and "No" indicates it does not meet the test of Just Cause.

Circle correct answer "Yes" or "No."

Situations

1. An employee was one hour late to work one time, and, as a result, was suspended without pay for one day.

   Yes   No

2. An employee, born in France, was observed drinking a glass of wine while eating lunch on college property during the workday. She claimed she did not realize there was a rule against drinking wine with her meal because in her culture wine is considered part of the food. She was terminated.

   Yes   No

3. Two employees called in sick and went to a Mariner baseball game that started at noon. The president of the college board saw them at the game and reported them to the president. One employee had two years experience and a clean record with no discipline. The second employee worked in the college for twenty years and was an Association activist who was viewed as a "thorn in the side of Management." The president docked the two-year employee one day's pay and the twenty-year employee was docked five day's pay because he should have known better. Also, both received a letter of reprimand in their personnel file.

   Yes   No

4. A member was accused of sexual harassment by students in her classes. After college officials interviewed several students, she was suspended with pay pending a trial date. She claimed she should have received an oral warning as the first step in discipline and not been suspended.

   Yes   No

5. A faculty member and her secretary were ordered by their dean to search students after a telephone call alerted the college a disgruntled student had a small homemade pipe bomb. The employees refused. The dean wrote each a letter of reprimand for failure to comply with an order. They both filed a separate grievance.

   Yes   No

JUST CAUSE FINAL EXAM 10 ANSWERS
FACULTY AND ALL CLASSIFIED

Answering "Yes" means it meets the standards and guidelines of Just Cause
and "No" indicates it does not meet the test of Just Cause.

Circle correct answer "Yes" or "No."

Situations

1. An employee was one hour late to work one time, and, as a result, was suspended without pay for one day.

    Yes   **No**

2. An employee, born in France, was observed drinking a glass of wine while eating lunch on college property during the workday. She claimed she did not realize there was a rule against drinking wine with her meal because in her culture wine is considered part of the food. She was terminated.

    Yes   **No**

3. Two employees called in sick and went to a Mariner baseball game that started at noon. The president of the college board saw them at the game and reported them to the president. One employee had two years experience and a clean record with no discipline. The second employee worked in the college for twenty years and was an Association activist who was viewed as a "thorn in the side of Management." The president docked the two-year employee one day's pay and the twenty-year employee was docked five day's pay because he should have known better. Also, both received a letter of reprimand in their personnel file.

    Yes   **No**

4. A member was accused of sexual harassment by students in her classes after college officials interviewed several students. She was suspended with pay pending a trial date. She claimed she should have received an oral warning as the first step in discipline and not been suspended.

    Yes   No

5. A faculty member and her secretary were ordered by their dean to search students after a telephone call alerted the college a disgruntled student had a small homemade pipe bomb. The employees refused. The dean wrote each a letter of reprimand for failure to comply with an order. They both filed a separate grievance.

    Yes   **No**

JUST CAUSE:
THE MOST IMPORTANT TEST

1. The last and most important standard of Just Cause: Did the grievant do what is alleged?

2. In 80% of the cases, arbitrators in Just Cause cases based their decision on the last standard.

3. The Association's strongest case is when it proves the grievant did not do what is alleged.

4. The best arguments and most persuasive testimony clearly demonstrate the accusations are false.

5. The Association has to make and win its case through its own witnesses so trying to win your case through cross-examination of Management witnesses in "Perry Mason" style is generally not successful.

6. Witness testimony is compelling and credible by having direct knowledge such as the following:

    The witness:

    > a. witnessed the event firsthand.
    > b. remembers the event.
    > c. can clearly describe and explain the event.
    > d. has a wealth of recollection about the event.

7. Trying to win a Just Cause case based on procedural issues is very risky and probably not winnable.

JUST CAUSE CONTINUUM

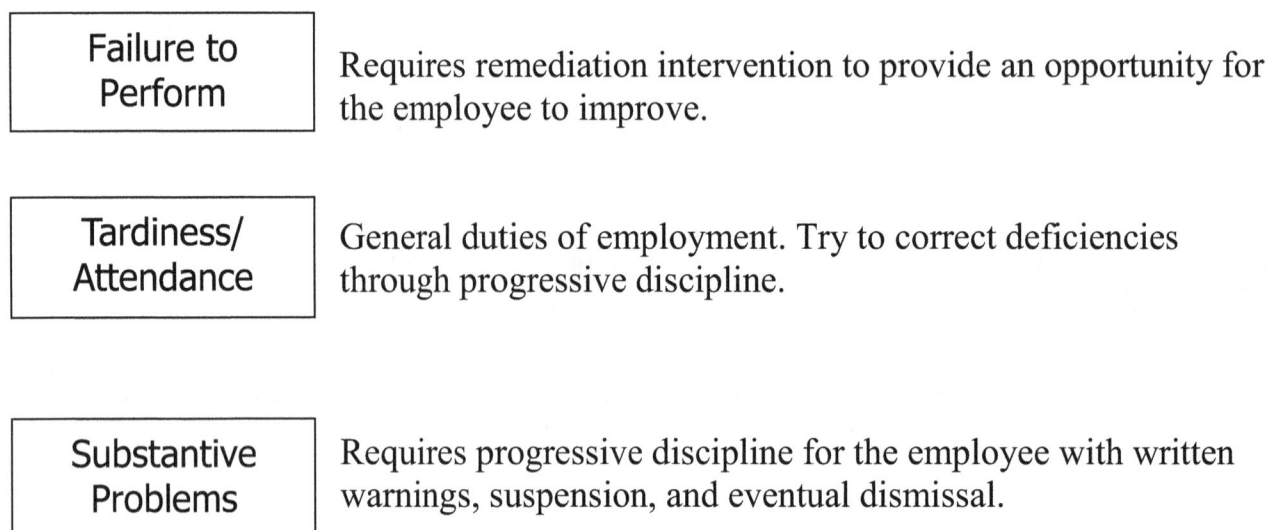

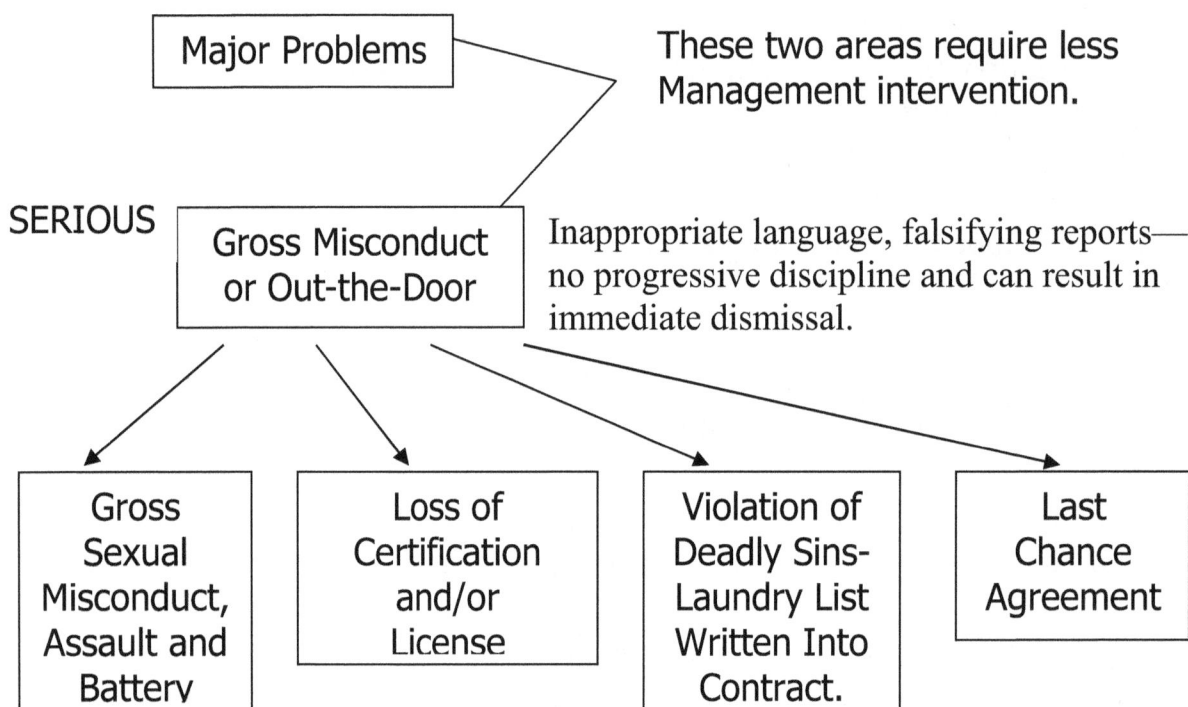

| Failure to Perform | Requires remediation intervention to provide an opportunity for the employee to improve. |

| Tardiness/ Attendance | General duties of employment. Try to correct deficiencies through progressive discipline. |

| Substantive Problems | Requires progressive discipline for the employee with written warnings, suspension, and eventual dismissal. |

Major Problems — These two areas require less Management intervention.

SERIOUS

| Gross Misconduct or Out-the-Door | Inappropriate language, falsifying reports— no progressive discipline and can result in immediate dismissal. |

| Gross Sexual Misconduct, Assault and Battery | Loss of Certification and/or License | Violation of Deadly Sins- Laundry List Written Into Contract. | Last Chance Agreement |

Gross Stupidity Rule = Assault and Battery, Sexual Misconduct; if proven, can result in immediate dismissal.

Employees must be informed about the rules beforehand, and potential consequences of violations.

JUST CAUSE CASE 11
K–12 EDUCATORS AND CLASSIFIED

A long-time educator's significant other, who was employed at the same education enterprise as a gardener/landscaper, was arrested for having a small-scale marijuana-growing operation powered by a sophisticated flood light system in a barn which, according to him, was strictly for personal consumption. Management fired both of them. She wanted to appeal based on the operation was the sole responsibility of her husband; she had nothing to do with it and had no knowledge. He said the operation had no bearing on his ability to do the job. Both had excellent evaluations and no previous disciplinary action. He also stated she had no knowledge of his "marijuana-growing operation." She believed he had an "indoor garden/nursery" in the barn. She claimed never to have visited the barn, which was located twenty miles from their home, in a very remote area. They worked in a major urban area, but lived fifty miles from the city in a very small isolated town.

The Association appealed their cases to arbitration. The employees were in different bargaining units but were represented by the same state organization. Their contracts had a standard Just Cause provision.

Was the Just Cause provision violated?

Strategy recommendation for the Association:

Prepare a list of Association arguments for the case.

JUST CAUSE CASE 11
ANSWER

The arbitrators upheld the grievances in both cases.

List possible reasons why?

JUST CAUSE CASE 12
FACULTY AND CLASSIFIED

A new marine science faculty member, who as part of her job responsibility provides operating instructions for piloting the boat on the water during the workday, tested positive for marijuana. Her significant other is a retired United Airlines airplane mechanic responsible for maintaining the college airplane. He also tested positive for marijuana. They were suspended without pay for five days. They argued "passive ingestion" because they worked as bouncers at his brother's local nightclub on weekends and had to go into the restrooms and evict patrons who were smoking marijuana. While they were performing their weekend job, they passively ingested some of the smoke.

They are members of their respective local Associations that are affiliated with the same state and national organization.

They were reinstated after the five-day suspension. The contract had a standard Just Cause provision.

Was the just cause provision violated?

Strategy recommendation for the Association:

Prepare a list of the Association arguments for the case.

When finished refer to discussion on page 44.

JUST CAUSE CASE 13
K–12 EDUCATORS AND CLASSIFIED

A new driver education teacher, who as part of her job responsibility provides the operating instructions in the car during the workday, tested positive for marijuana. Her significant other was also a driver-education teaching assistant. He also tested positive for marijuana. They were suspended without pay for five days. They argued "passive ingestion" because they worked as bouncers at his brother's local nightclub on weekends and had to go into the restrooms and evict patrons who were smoking marijuana. While they were performing their weekend job, they passively ingested some of the smoke.

They are members of their respective local Associations that are affiliated with the same state and national organization.

They were reinstated after the five-day suspension. The contract had a standard Just Cause provision.

Was the just cause provision violated?

Strategy recommendation for the Association:

Prepare a list of Association arguments for the case to advocate for the members.

When finished refer to discussion on page 44.

JUST CAUSE CASES 12 AND 13
ANSWER

The Arbitrator denied the grievance.

List possible reasons why?

Have a discussion about driving vehicles, operating equipment, and handling of hazardous materials having an impact on the arbitrator's decision.

Have a discussion about employees should have known better, especially if they are aware future job-required tests are part of their employment responsibilities.

ADVOCACY SCENARIO 14
K–12 EDUCATORS AND CLASSIFIED

A young male high school assistant was working as a volunteer at a local youth club.

This past weekend when the club's senior group went on a field trip to the state capitol, the assistant served as a supervisor.

The group remained overnight at a hotel near the capitol building.

The assistant did, in fact, provide alcoholic beverages to four of the boys in the group that evening in his hotel room. Two of the boys were students of the assistant.

After leaving the assistant's room, the boys became rowdy in the halls and were confronted by the club's director.

The director discovered from the boys the assistant had provided them the liquor.

Early Sunday morning the director called the superintendent and informed him of the incident.

On Monday morning the superintendent called the assistant into his office and summarily suspended him without pay for six weeks. He works half time as a teacher and the other half as a paraprofessional and is a member of both bargaining units.

The assistant wants to fight the suspension.

While he admits to giving the boys the liquor, his position is that (a) he undertook the club work voluntarily and (b) what he did was in no way related to his employment with the school and he therefore should not be subject to employment discipline for this non-job-related action.

Exercise is on the next page.

ADVOCACY SCENARIO14 EXERCISE SHEET

The Association strategy recommendation:

Reasons:

Start a discussion about outside employment having an impact on your job. Are educators different? If yes, then why?

WEINGARTEN RIGHTS

IT IS THE RIGHT OF AN EMPLOYEE TO THE PRESENCE OF AN ASSOCIATION REPRESENTATIVE AT A MEETING WITH THE EMPLOYER IF THERE IS REASONABLE EXPECTATION DISCIPLINE MAY RESULT.

The following are key concepts regarding Weingarten rights:

1.   The right to representation only comes when the employee requests it. Management does not have to advise you of your right to representation.

2.   An employee may not unilaterally leave the interview to seek representation contrary to the supervisor's orders.

3.   An employer cannot require substituting one designated Association Representative for another representative.

4.   Time should be provided to consult with your representative before the investigating meeting.

5.   The right to representation exists even if investigated by an outside agency and/or person.

6.   The right to a representative only applies in situations where an employee *reasonably* expects disciplinary action could result.

7.   The employer has no duty to bargain with any Association Representative attending the investigating interview.

When an employee is disciplined for exercising Weingarten rights, there are remedies that can be sought. Also remember, if the supervisor wants to meet with you, ask what is the purpose of the meeting? Then decide if you should have Association Representation!

WEINGARTEN RIGHTS
QUIZ 15

TRUE or FALSE? Circle the correct answer
+ for True or **O** for False

1. Management is not required to advise you of
    your right to representation.   +   or   **O**

2. An employee does not have the option of
    leaving an interview to seek Association
    Representation when Management says he or   +   or   **O**
    she cannot leave.

3. An employer has the option of selecting a
    designated Association Representative.   +   or   **O**

4. Management does not have to provide you
    with time to meet with your Association
    Representative before the investigating   +   or   **O**
    meeting.

5. The employee has no right to representation
    when being investigated by an outside agency.   +   or   **O**

6. The right to representation applies where an
    employee can reasonably expect disciplinary
    action could result.   +   or   **O**

WEINGARTEN RIGHTS
QUIZ 15 ANSWERS

TRUE or FALSE? Circle the correct answer
+ for True or **O** for False

1. Management is not required to advise you of your right to representation.   <u>+</u>   or   **O**

2. An employee does not have the option of leaving an interview to seek Association Representation when Management says he or she cannot leave.   <u>+</u>   or   **O**

3. An employer has the option of selecting a designated Association Representative.   +   or   **<u>O</u>**

4. Management does not have to provide you with time to meet with your Association Representative before the investigating meeting.   +   or   **<u>O</u>**

5. The employee has no right to representation when being investigated by an outside agency.   +   or   **<u>O</u>**

6. The right to representation applies where an employee can reasonably expect disciplinary action could result.   <u>+</u>   or   **O**

GUIDELINES FOR AN ADMINISTRATIVE MEETING

❖ Be cordial since you have an official role.

❖ Conduct yourself in a professional manner.

❖ Advise the administrator your role is to represent the member.

❖ Sit close to the employee.

❖ Listen carefully.

❖ Take notes recording direct statements, making notes of the time, place, those present and their titles, and the starting and ending time of the meeting.

❖ Request copies of any documentation shown or referenced in the meeting.

❖ Use the following if necessary: "We will take this under advisement;" or "Give us time to think about it;" or "We'll get back to you on this matter."

❖ The objective is discovery; to gather as much information as possible.

❖ Silence is golden—do not feel the pressure to respond—utilize dead-space strategy when appropriate.

ADVICE TO MEMBERS BEFORE
ATTENDING A MANAGEMENT MEETING

1. Ask if the meeting could lead to disciplinary action. If the answer is yes, state you want representation and excuse yourself until such time.

2. Tell the truth.

3. If you cannot remember, say, "I do not remember."

4. If you have partial recall, say, "To the best of my recollection this is what happened…."

5. If you are not certain about the answer to a question, give a similar response.

6. When asked a question, answer the question as briefly as possible.

WHAT TO DO UNTIL HELP ARRIVES

1. DON'T RESIGN. Once Management accepts your resignation, it generally cancels any rights you might otherwise exercise.

2. DON'T SIGN ANYTHING UNDER PRESSURE. Do not be coerced into signing anything when you are under a time demand or otherwise pressured. Politely refuse and indicate you need time to make an informed decision.

3. GET IT IN WRITING. Any agreements you reach with Management or any proposals, statements or utterances received through the Management's Representative(s) should be reduced to writing. If Management refused to provide written documentation, you should write down the understandings reached and deliver a copy to the other Party.

4. CONTACT THE ASSOCIATION. As the Association Representative, you should be able to represent the member and be present at all meetings between the member and Management.

The member should take some time before giving a commitment or making a final decision when faced with an employment crisis.

WHAT TO DO IN A DIRE EMERGENCY

1. When contacted by security, law enforcement, or a supervisor concerning a work-related matter about criminal issues such as assault and battery, harassment, or sexual abuse:
   a. Make no statement to anyone.
   b. Contact your professional Association Advocate and/or attorney immediately.

2. When faced with a dangerous situation at work that threatens substantial bodily injury or poses a significant health hazard:
   a. Contact your supervisor.
   b. Move away from any hazardous area.
   c. Notify Risk Management or equivalent.
   d. If you become sick at work, inform your supervisor you need to go home.
   e. If necessary, file a workers' compensation claim.

3. In case you are assaulted at work:
   a. Report the incident to Management.
   b. File a complaint with law enforcement.
   c. File a workers' compensation claim.

WHAT AN ADVOCATE SHOULD KNOW ABOUT
INSUBORDINATION

YOU CAN BE FIRED

1.   Insubordination is one of the major factors in dismissals and is one of the easiest charges to prove.

WHO'S BOSS

1.   Managers have some Management Rights simply because they are the "boss."

2.   Supervisors have the right to exert leadership, to direct the institutional operations, to enforce rules, policies, reasonable orders and directions so long as they conform to the contract and are clear and unambiguous, not injurious to your health, applied uniformly, and justly administered.

DEFINITION

1.   Insubordination is defined as "failure to obey authority."

2.   If an employee comes to you and questions a directive issued by the immediate supervisor, advise the member to discuss the objections with the supervisor.

3.   If the supervisor insists the order be obeyed, advise the member to comply unless there is a threat to the health or safety of the staff, the member or others.

4.   A member may ask for the "order" to be in writing.

5.   The supervisor does _NOT_ have to put it in writing in order to later claim you were insubordinate for failure to carry out the order.

WORK THEN GRIEVE

The member can file a grievance.
This is the "work then grieve" rule.

INSUBORDINATION QUIZ 16
ALL TRAINEES

Does this constitute insubordination?
Circle Yes or No.

1. A member refused to perform a routine job. Her manager ordered her to complete the task. She demanded the order in writing. He refused to put the order in writing. She refused the work. The manager disciplined her for insubordination.

    YES or **NO**

2. A member refused a new assignment. The supervisor ordered him to do it. He hesitated for a brief time before complying. The supervisor wrote a letter of reprimand for insubordination.

    YES or **NO**

3. A member of the bargaining unit in a position of authority ordered another member to complete a normal task. The member refused and the other member reported him to the supervisor. The supervisor disciplined the member who disobeyed for insubordination.

    YES or **NO**

INSUBORDINATION QUIZ 16
ANSWERS

Does this constitute insubordination?
Circle Yes or No.

1. A member refused to perform a routine job. Her manager ordered her to complete the task. She demanded the order in writing. He refused to put the order in writing. She refused the work. The manager disciplined her for insubordination.　　**YES** or **NO**

2. A member refused a new assignment. The supervisor ordered him to do it. He hesitated for a brief time, before complying. The supervisor wrote a letter of reprimand for insubordination.　　**YES** or **NO**

3. A member of the bargaining unit in a position of authority ordered another member to complete a normal task. The member refused and the other member reported him to the supervisor. The supervisor disciplined the member who disobeyed for insubordination.　　**YES** or **NO**

INSUBORDINATION SCENARIO 17
K–12 EDUCATORS AND CLASSIFIED

The principal orders the school evacuated because of flooding in the basement caused by an old, overheated boiler. First she orders all the female staff, educators and classified to monitor students in the playground. Secondly, she orders all the male staff, classified and educators, to go to the basement and remove important, sensitive, and confidential school records stored near the boiler before it potentially explodes.

Representatives of both the male and female staff ask you, the Association President, what to do because the principal has threatened to discipline anyone for insubordination who does not cooperate.

1. What advice do you give to the employees?

2. Devise a representation strategy for a mass discipline meeting.

INSUBORDINATION SCENARIO 18
ALL FACULTY AND CLASSIFIED

A volatile student who was recently suspended with a restraining order from being on college property for threatening other students has returned to campus brandishing a weapon. The dean orders all staff, both faculty and classified, to search the buildings for the deranged student in order for the teaching and learning process to resume.

The staff asks you as an Association Representative what to do because the dean has threatened to discipline any employee for insubordination who does not cooperate.

1. What advice do you have for the employees?

2. Devise a representation strategy for a mass discipline meeting.

ADVOCACY CASE 19
K–12 EDUCATORS AND CLASSIFIED

An employee had been disciplined several times for using bad language in her classroom and received a three-day suspension without pay after the last incident. The Association, Management and the employee signed a "Last Chance Agreement" stating that any further offenses of a similar nature would result in immediate and final dismissal. A supervisor sitting in the stands at an away football game heard the same employee yelling "foul language" at the other team during the game. Other employees present said the remarks were "on the edge" but there was no "foul language." The employee claimed it was an off-work incident by a citizen and not in any capacity as an employee and it was a first amendment right to express her views of the officiating during the game.

The employee was terminated Monday morning with no face-to-face communication with Management.

The employee is a half-time educator and half-time paraprofessional who belongs to both the teacher and classified bargaining units represented by the same state and national organization. The Agreement had a standard Just Cause clause.

The Associations appealed the case to arbitration.

Was the Just Cause provision violated?

List the Association arguments.

ADVOCACY CASE 20
FACULTY AND CLASSIFIED

An employee, who works directly with students every day, was disciplined several times for using bad language in his work area and received a three-day suspension without pay after the last incident. The Association, the college and the employee signed a "Last Chance Agreement" stating that any further offenses of a similar nature would result in immediate and final dismissal. The college board president was sitting in the stands at a home basketball game heard the same employee making loud "inappropriate comments" directed at the other team during the game. Other employees present said the remarks were "on the edge" but there was no "foul language." The employee was terminated Monday morning with no face-to-face communication with Management. The member claimed it was an off-work incident by a citizen and not in any capacity as a school employee. The contract contained a standard Just Cause provision.

The Association appealed the case to arbitration.

Was the Just Cause provision violated?

Prepare a list of Association arguments for the case.

SEVEN WAYS TO SAY "NO"
THE POWER OF "NO"*

1. Say "No, No, No."

2. Our members will not accept this settlement proposal. "No."

3. We cannot in good conscience recommend this grievance settlement to our members. "No."

4. Our answer to this is still "No."

5. This is unacceptable. "No."

6. This proposed grievance settlement represents a lesser standard than our current agreement. "No."

7. This grievance settlement offer does not meet what is granted in the contract and agreed to at the bargaining table. "No."

* It is all right to say "No" when appropriate and there is no need to apologize or feel bad about saying "No."

ONE WAY TO SAY
"NO"
UTILIZING DEAD-SPACE STRATEGY

NO RESPONSE

"NO" is the single most powerful
word/response in advocacy
and/or conflict resolution.

There is power in silence.

REPRESENTATION EXERCISE 21
FACULTY

An employee, who taught business law and business ethics, was convicted of a felony for running an illegal bookmaking operation out of his home. The college called him for a meeting after he received a one-year suspended sentence and three years of probation. He contacted the Association and demanded to file a grievance if there was discipline because there was no written rule or policy against this type of activity.

The same night of the conviction he was also given a ticket for drunk driving. The member claimed he was innocent because the police were "out to get him" since he was a high-profile citizen. He claimed he was innocent of the driving charge and a jury trial was scheduled the next month. He said he gargled with Listerine® before leaving home and the policewoman assumed she smelled alcohol on his breath. At the time, he also had an inner ear infection that caused him to stumble when he walked.

The college fired him after the driving charge. The member and his Advocate scheduled a meeting with Management to dispute the firing. The college argued it was not necessary to list all offenses that result in dismissal since it was generally covered by the standard Just Cause provision in the contract.

Devise a representation strategy.

Prepare Association arguments for the Management meeting.

REPRESENTATION EXERCISE 22
K–12 EDUCATORS AND CLASSIFIED

A twenty-year employee with a clean record was given a ticket for drunk driving. The member claimed she was innocent because the "politically motivated" police were "out to get her" since she was a high-profile citizen. She was immediately released after refusing to take the test because she feared the police were going to "set her up." She claimed she was innocent of the driving charge and a jury trial was scheduled for the next month. She claimed she gargled with Listerine® before leaving home and the policeman mistakenly assumed he smelled alcohol on her breath. At the time, she also had an inner ear infection that caused her to stumble when she walked. She worked half time as a computer teacher and half time as a computer technician. She was a dual member of both the educator and classified bargaining units.

Management fired her for the driving charge. The member and her Advocate scheduled a meeting with Management to dispute the firing.

Prepare arguments for the Management meeting.

REPRESENTATION EXERCISE 23
ALL TRAINEES

Joan Tardee calls you, the Association Representative, and claims her supervisor is harassing her. The supervisor claims she was late several times in the last year but has no documentation. She admits to being a few minutes late on occasion, but she says she walked in with other employees at the same time. The supervisor said he talked to one other employee about being late. In the event he discovers others, he will talk to them individually. Also, if we will provide the names of the employees, he will contact them and deal with their tardiness in an appropriate manner.

Joan tells you her young children were sick at home and she had to wait until her mother arrived before leaving for work. The late practice at the site is to call and notify the office of the emergency and the anticipated time of arrival. She did not notify anyone since she always makes up the time by working through her breaks, lunchtime, and, if necessary, works extra time after regular hours.

1.   Devise a written strategy to present arguments to fairly represent the member in a Management meeting.

2.   Develop some ideas to advise Joan what to do in the future under these same circumstances.

BASIC TENETS OF "VOICE" WHEN MAKING DECISIONS: THE BEST WAY TO GET TO "YES"

1. The stakeholder Parties determine the composition and number of representatives from each constituent group.

2. Our members have a seat with authentic participation and a real voice in the decision-making process.

3. Our Association selects its own representatives.

4. Our members have an equal or significant (majority) voice in decision making.

5. Our members are present and participate in the final decisions.

6. The decision-making climate is free of fear and intimidation.

7. If a consensus model is used and consensus is reached, all Parties agree to support the decision and work toward implementation.

8. If you are either late or absent, you consent.

9. The process always moves forward and will not be revisited for anyone for any reason.

10. The first order of business is to agree on a decision-making process, which cannot be changed.

Litmus Test for Voice and Accountability

1. Did we have a voice throughout the entire decision making process?

2. If not, why not?

3. There can be no expectation of member accountability if we did not have a voice.

BASIC TENETS OF VOICE
QUIZ 24

Circle words appropriate for the basic tenets of voice.

1. Unilateral

2. Participation

3. Fear

4. Self Select

5. Equal

6. Intimidation

7. Consensus

8. Collaborative

9. Authoritarian

10. Fair Process

BASIC TENETS OF VOICE
QUIZ 24 ANSWERS

Circle words appropriate for the basic tenets of voice.

1. Unilateral

2. | **Participation** |

3. Fear

4. | **Self Select** |

5. | **Equal** |

6. Intimidation

7. | **Consensus** |

8. | **Collaborative** |

9. Authoritarian

10. | **Fair Process** |

LACK OF COOPERATION AS AN ORGANIZING STRATEGY
EDUCATORS

1. This is the flipside or opposite of voice.

2. In the event, Management does not want to recognize our voice; one option is to not cooperate with them in making decisions to run the enterprise.

3. Refusing to cooperate is a powerful organizing strategy because it is virtually impossible to effectively and efficiently administer programs without our cooperation.

4. A community-college administration tried to operate the educational program without department chairs. The faculty Association and college were unsuccessful in bargaining terms and conditions of employment for department chairs. The Association agreed the college could hire an administrator to do the work of the department chairs. It was a complete failure because the college made poor decisions that resulted in chaos and confusion.

5. There are some decisions Management will have the final authority over, either by contract or by statute, such as tenure, hiring, etc. If we have a voice in the decisions, but Management has the final decision, then our expectation is our decisions should be honored like "Ivory® soap", which is 99 44/100% pure.

6. If not, we should demand written reasons for denial. If Management presents new information and/or valid reasons, the committee should review its original decision and make a new recommendation.

7. If Management refuses to give reasons or gives unacceptable reasons, then we should refuse to cooperate in the decision. In short, we inform them of our decision and any new process will be done without our voice.

8. Ground rules for the process: if Management tells the committee to make three choices and the committee only finds one candidate acceptable, then pass one name on to the employer; if Management says three, and we find two equally acceptable, then pass two names to Management.

9. In short, do not allow administrators who are far away from the decision to influence our decisions. The best decisions are made closest to where the work is performed by the people performing the work.

10. We must assert ourselves and say "NO" when decisions or rules are made that are not in our best interests.

ADVOCACY PROBLEM 25
ALL TRAINEES

A member took a day of sick leave and went duck hunting.

Upon her return and while she was in the lounge, a colleague welcomed her back and expressed the hope she was feeling better.

The member said she was duck hunting. Her manager was in the lounge at the time, but not immediately seen by the member.

After hearing the member's comment, the manager walked up to her and asked her if she had shot any ducks.

The member said "No", and the manager left.

No other persons heard this conversation.

The manager docked the member's pay for an unauthorized absence.

The member has now come to you and asks for support and representation in filing a grievance.

She said she was duck hunting, but was going to stand by her story she was ill.

She said the burden was on Management to prove she was not sick, and it was "his word against mine."

How should the Association reply to the member's request?

Strategy recommendation:

Rationale for decision:

WHAT TO DO FOR MEMBER-TO-MEMBER DISPUTES

Strategies for any type of problem:

1. Advise the complaining member to meet with the other member face-to-face to discuss the problem.

2. Have an Association Representative go with the complaining member to meet with the other member and discuss the problem.

3. The Association Representative alone can meet with the other member(s) and discuss the problem.

4. Find some other appropriate way of delivering the message.

5. In the event there is a "cease and desist" message, the Association Representative can be the messenger.

6. Assign an Association Representative to each member and meet with the Parties to resolve the problem.

7. Some combination of 1–5 should be attempted prior to going to Management.

ADVOCACY PROBLEM 26
ALL TRAINEES

Two employees have been engaged in a long term simmering dispute. An ugly verbal confrontation occurred between the employees at work in full view of several other employees.

One employee is in his first year of employment. The second is a twenty-year employee who has been an Association activist and past president for several years. The new employee wants to file a grievance against the senior employee.

Assume that you are going to advise your Association's grievance committee, who are faced with deciding which position the Association should take on the request.

Consider and analyze the matter fully and decide the appropriate Association strategy.

Rationale for decision.

REMEMBER THE IRON RULE

Never do for others what they can do for themselves!

GRIEVANCES, COMPLAINTS, GRIPING, AND WHINING

Grievances:

A grievance is an alleged violation of either the facts, interpretation, uniform application, or application of the language specific to the facts or intent of the Agreement.

Complaints:

A complaint is an allegation by one or more employees stating a policy, practice or procedure has either been violated or not evenly applied, or unfair treatment has occurred not covered by the Agreement.

Griping:

A gripe is a non-contract complaint by a person or persons who disagree, and is, at times, for the purpose of seriously irritating others in the workplace.

Whining:

A whiner is a person who constantly and continually complains about many things in front of others for the purpose of "stirring the pot" in order to create problems and/or unrest among other employees.

GRIEVANCE ADJUDICATION BACKGROUND

1. Historically speaking, prior to the rise of Unions, Management Rights were unencumbered in the treatment of employees.

2. Management could make changes at its sole discretion.

3. Collective Bargaining limited employer rights in managing employees.

4. Grievance procedures were born as an inexpensive method of enforcing the limitations placed on Management.

5. The first *quid pro quo* trades made at the bargaining table were employees who won binding arbitration of grievances and Management obtained "no-strike clauses" and, as a result, "labor peace," since early disputes, at times, resulted in "wildcat strikes."

6. Grievances pertain to contract matters to the extent allowed by the grievance procedure.

7. Contracts without binding arbitration are limited to court enforcement, which is expensive and time consuming.

8. Contracts with binding arbitration but which exclude important provisions are limited.

9. Normally, clauses/issues/items in the Agreement are grievable.

10. Clear/unambiguous language will prevail over unclear language.

11. Specific language will supersede over general language.

12. Language that mentions a group, or portions thereof, and is silent on others will mean others are excluded.

13. Mandatory language with "shall' is more compelling than permissive language with "may."

14. The contract will be viewed "as a whole" in order to give meaning to all its parts during review of contract language so one definition will apply to all provisions.

15. The "Intent of the Parties" at the table is critical, especially if there is to be a "meeting of the minds."

16. Absent all or some of the above, Past Practice is compelling.

GRIEVANCE FACTS OF LIFE

All grievances should include the following:

1. Who has the grievance?

2. What is the complaint and impact on the member(s)?

3. When did it happen?

4. Where did it happen?

5. Why is it a grievance and which contract sections violated?

6. Are Past Practices involved?

7. Remedy sought to correct violation?

8. All impacted Parties "made whole."

9. Remedy must conform to other parts of contract.

10. The grievance, *in Toto*, should be self-explanatory.

A VALID GRIEVANCE

1. Falls within the scope of the grievance procedure.

2. Is timely.

3. Is valid and winnable.

4. Is in the appropriate venue for resolution.

5. The overall long-term impact in a win is positive.

6. The Duty of Fair Representation has not been violated.

7. No reasonable settlement is possible.

8. The grievance is justified for some reason such as organizational, future bargaining, organizing, community, and/or public relations.

9. Management has not followed the basic tenets of due process and/or Just Cause.

WHY HAVE A GRIEVANCE PROCEDURE?

1. It provides a safe, mutually endorsed, systematic way to resolve problems.

2. It is a way to interpret the Agreement.

3. It provides an opportunity to explain our position.

4. It establishes our members' rights.

5. It provides records for the next negotiations.

6. It established a way to resolve problems at the first step.

ASK DR. GRIEVE 27
ALL TRAINEES

The following situations have been submitted for your review and analysis. Provide an appropriate response based on your knowledge of advocacy, your Agreement, and any grievance experience. Answer the best you can, based on your knowledge and experience level.

1. There is a drive-by sniper scare at your work site. Your supervisor asks you to go to the front of the building to get a description of the driver and/or the license-plate number in order to save lives. What should you do?

2. Your supervisor always has someone from the president's office with her when she hears grievances. Can she do this?

3. I filed a step-one grievance in writing and the supervisor said it was not valid because I did not attempt to resolve the problem informally first. What should I do now?

4. Management deducted a day's pay from my check nine months ago; I believe it was in error. Can I still file a grievance?

5. I asked my supervisor to tell me how he settled a complaint by Ms. Roman who did not want me to represent her. He refused. Is he required to tell Grievance Representatives the resolution of informal complaints?

6. Mr. Smith does not want to appeal her grievance to step two, but I think it is important. Can the Association appeal?

7. Management misplaced a member on the salary schedule. The member discovered the error six months later and wanted to file a grievance but Management said it was beyond the ten-day timeline.

8. I investigated a potential grievance with an employee during my fifteen-minute break in the lunchroom. Management said I have to investigate grievances after work. Is this correct?

ASK DR. GRIEVE 27
TRAINER NOTES

1. Refuse to comply on grounds it would endanger your safety.

2. YES. In most cases.

3. YES. If timeliness is a problem, simply advance the grievance to the next step without a response from Management.

4. What is the time limit for initiating grievances? In most cases failure to file a grievance within the time limits will invalidate the grievance. A one-time pay deduction is not a continuing grievance. A dispute over placement on the salary schedule that results in misplacement, over and over again, is considered a continuing grievance beginning with each pay period.

5. It is generally understood the bargaining agent has the responsibility to ensure the Agreement is not violated. It is also understood Management cannot settle a grievance that violates the contractual rights of others. In order to live up to the Association's responsibility, Management is required to provide the information.

6. An individual generally has the right to process grievances without the assistance of the Association through the pre-arbitration steps of the procedure. If an individual does not wish to continue a grievance and the Association can file a grievance on its own, the grievance can continue to be advanced. Only the Association can take grievances to arbitration. Even if the individual grievant wants to go to arbitration, the Association is not obligated to do so as long as the reason for not going to arbitration is neither arbitrary nor discriminatory and does not violate the Association's duty to fairly represent.

7. This falls under the category of a continuing or recurring grievance when timelines are retriggered every time a member is paid in error (a new-day timeline starts).

8. Break and lunchtime are generally considered non-duty time belonging to employees. Generally, Management has control of preparation time for educators.

GENERAL ADVOCACY 28 QUIZ
ALL TRAINEES

A for Agree   **D** for Disagree   **?** Not Sure

1. Well-paid employees are less likely to have their rights violated. ____

2. Employee rights can be effectively safeguarded with an effective grievance procedure. ____

3. The Grievance Committee should initiate grievance against other employees. ____

4. The Association should judge all grievances on merits before filing them. ____

5. The Association is responsible for processing grievances for all bargaining unit members. ____

6. All information related to employee discipline is confidential. ____

7. The final factor to determine whether or not to support a grievance is the majority vote of an Association opinion survey. ____

8. The Grievance Committee is an impartial Party in resolving grievances. ____

9. An employee advocate should search out and discover contract violations. ____

10. The Association should represent employees whether right or wrong. ____

11. Grievance-procedure decisions are the exclusive responsibility of the Association. ____

GENERAL ADVOCACY 28 QUIZ
ANSWERS

1. D
2. A
3. D
4. D
5. A
6. A
7. D
8. D
9. A
10. A
11. D

ASSOCIATION CODE OF CONDUCT

I will not criticize any colleague except to the individual directly.

If any colleague is being criticized in my presence, *I will* confront the criticism and ask that it stop.

I will not participate in any conversations with Management that criticize or negatively speculate about any colleague.

I will settle my differences with colleagues within the Association.

I will engage in debate, offer others every opportunity for debate, and respect minority viewpoints, but *I will* observe and support the majority mandate of the Association.

ASK DR. ADVOCATE 29
ALL EDUCATORS

The following situations have been submitted for your review and analysis. Provide an appropriate response based on your knowledge of processing grievances and the provisions of your Collective Bargaining Agreement.

1. Do days when employees are present but students are not count as "days" in the grievance procedure?

2. There is a member-to-member dispute. You are representing Member A. Member B requests you represent her also. What is your strategy?

3. An event occurred forty-five days prior to filing a grievance. The grievant received knowledge ten days ago. The Agreement has a ten-day window for filing grievances. Does this grievance fall within the timelines?

4. I filed a grievance and won. I discovered a record of the grievance in my personnel file. Do I have a second grievance?

5. I asked a manager for some records pertinent to a pending grievance. She refused to provide the data citing confidentiality. What is my next move?

6. The Association Representative's mother was sick. She was on family illness leave and missed a timeline. What happens now?

7. I asked the Association Representative to be present at Level I. The manager denied her access to the meeting. What are my options?

8. A fee payer (nonmember) brought his attorney to Level II. I asked the supervisor to demand the lawyer leave; she refused. Who was right?

ASK DR. ADVOCATE 29
TRAINER NOTES

1. Employee workdays, unless otherwise specified, normally are the rule. However, it depends on the local contract.

2. Refer to mediation service.

3. YES. Within ten days of knowledge.

4. YES. Must be in separate file.

5. Management must provide relevant information.

6. Grievance denied; missed timeline.

7. Grievant has the right to representation.

8. Member has the right to bring own attorney strictly to observe. The Association is responsible for any meeting strategy and arbitration cases.

ASK DR. ADVOCATE 30
ALL CLASSIFIED

The following situations have been submitted for your review and analysis. Provide an appropriate response based on your knowledge of processing grievances and the provisions of your Collective Bargaining Agreement.

1. Do days when employees are on holiday count as "days" in the grievance procedure?

2. There is a member-to-member dispute. You are representing Member A. Member B requests you represent her also. What is your strategy?

3. An event occurred 45 days prior to filing a grievance. The grievant received knowledge 10 days ago. The Agreement has a ten-day window for filing grievances. Does this grievance fall within the timelines?

4. I filed a grievance and won. I discovered a record of the grievance in my personnel file. Do I have a second grievance?

5. I asked my Supervisor for some records pertinent to a pending grievance. She refused to provide the data regarding, citing confidentiality. What is my next move?

6. The Association Representative's mother was sick. She was on family illness leave and missed a timeline. What happens now?

7. I asked the Association Representative to be present at Level I. The Supervisor denied her access to the meeting. What are my options?

8. A Representation/Agency Fee Payer (non-member) brought his attorney to Level II. I asked the Supervisor to demand the lawyer leave. She refused. Who was right?

ASK DR. ADVOCATE 30
TRAINER NOTES

1. Employee workdays, unless otherwise specified, normally are the rule. However, it depends on the local contract.

2. Refer to mediation service.

3. YES. Within 30 days of knowledge.

4. YES. Must be in separate file.

5. Management must provide relevant information.

6. Grievance denied, missed timeline.

7. Grievant has the right to representation.

8. Member has the right to bring own attorney strictly to observe. Association is responsible for any meeting strategy and arbitration cases.

ADVOCACY SCENARIO 31
ALL TRAINEES

A member who has taken five weeks of sick leave is examined by a Management-appointed physician and certified as capable of returning to work.

The established practice on sick leaves of such length is to have a physician's approval of continued sick leave.

The member claims she is not ready and does not want to return to work. Her Manager orders her to return. She refuses and is dismissed.

The member wishes to file a grievance on the dismissal.

The Association has another physician examine the member and determined the member was not capable of returning to work.

Consider whether or not to support the grievance.

Discuss the dilemma and decide on a course of action on the next page.

ADVOCACY SCENARIO 31
EXERCISE SHEET

Strategy recommendation:

Reasons:

HOSTILE WORK ENVIRONMENT

ESSENTIAL COMPONENTS OF HOSTILE WORK ENVIRONMENT

The act or actions must be:

1. Severe.

2. Pervasive; continue over a long period of time.

    – or –

3. A single egregious act.

HOW TO FILE A HOSTILE WORK ENVIRONMENT COMPLAINT

1. File complaint with Management.

2. Management must take immediate corrective action once aware of the problem.

3. Management is required to investigate.

4. Management is required to communicate results of investigation in a timely manner.

5. If necessary, Management is required to take immediate corrective action.

MANAGEMENT RESPONSIBILITIES
[MANAGEMENT RIGHTS DEFINED]

1. Hire – Fire

2. Promote – Demote

3. Transfer – Involuntary Transfer

4. Discipline – Reward

5. Reprimand

6. Discharge – Dismiss

7. Suspend

8. Layoff – Recall

9. Assign – Direct (beyond routine)

10. Adjust Grievances

11. Evaluate

ADVOCACY CASE 32
ALL TRAINEES

Management suspects Rufus Christian of being under the influence of alcohol during the workday. The morning after the all-community centennial nighttime celebration, one of the supervisors observed Rufus "staggering on campus" while walking outside his work area. The supervisor did not confront him because she was too busy but called him into her office the next day and gave him a written reprimand for either drinking at/or right before work and suspended him for three days without pay. He explained he was acting as a "Good Samaritan" picking up trash leftover from the celebration the night before to clean up his work area and he had never in his life consumed alcohol.

He and the Association Advocate filed a just-cause discipline grievance.

Devise a representation strategy by designing a series of discovery questions.

Prepare arguments for a Level I grievance hearing.

ADVOCACY CASE 32
TRAINER NOTES

Trash and other types of debris are rarely distributed evenly on the ground. Consequently, the person picking up the trash oftentimes walks an irregular path to pick up the trash. As a result, it appeared the person was impaired, but actually was not, due to how the trash was located and the pattern of steps required to cleanup the area. The "burden of proof" is on Management.

QUESTIONING SKILLS
IN GRIEVANCE ADJUDICATION OR CONFLICT
RESOLUTION

THE MOST IMPORTANT PART OF CONFLICT RESOLUTION

Why Questioning?

1. A truly effective conflict resolution session involves both Parties asking and answering a series of questions to seek information.

2. Conflict resolution is not a speech and/or debate process; it involves intensive question and answer dialogue until there is a *"meeting of the minds."*

3. Listen! Skilled advocates are good listeners.

Useful Types of Questions

1. Open-ended questions seek information and allow for a wide variety of answers. Example: "What are your objections to our resolution?"

2. Closed-end questions invite a very limited response, typically a "yes" or "no." Closed-end questions are good for nailing down the intentions of the other Party or for bringing closure to a point or discussion. Examples: "Can we meet next Thursday at 4:00 p.m. at the Association office?" or, "Will Management support this grievance settlement agreement?"

3. Clarifying questions are generally follow-ups to open-ended questions. These questions seek additional information to bring clarity to a term or portion of the answer given by the other Party. When used properly, the result is more complete information about the intent of the other Party. Example: "When you say 'Last Chance Agreement,' what do you mean?"

4. Justifying questions challenge the other Party to explain how their proposed grievance settlement would be fairer, better, more practical, less costly, beneficial, etc. Example: "How would you expect employee trust to remain high if you do not abide by the intent of the Just Cause clause?"

5. "What if" questions—also called "supposals"—are used to explore possible compromises without officially committing to them. Often this is done in a "pencils down" session with no record keeping. Example: "If we agreed to accept your proposal to attend an anger management class, could you agree to keep the reprimand in the building file?"

QUESTIONING SKILLS EXERCISE 33

1.   Pair up with a trainee you do not know. Develop a series of open-ended questions to solicit as much background information as possible about the person you are interviewing for the first eight minutes.

2.   Record your answers.

3.   Use the last two minutes to ask as many closed-end and clarifying questions as possible to gain additional information about the person.

4.   At the end of the ten-minute interview, reverse the process.

Each trainee should calculate the total for the other trainee's interview of you by assigning one point for each major piece of information recorded. Each trainee will have a total number of points when the person was the first interviewer.

PAST PRACTICE CONCEPTS

Unwritten Clauses in the Agreement

1. This allows for resolution of ongoing contract interpretation problems.

2. This is caused by the complex nature of the employment relationship.

3. This is necessary because of ambiguous and uncertain contract language.

4. A Party cannot gain in arbitration what it failed to achieve at the bargaining table.

5. Evidence of true intent is crucial.

**PAST PRACTICE DEFINED**	_**KEY WORDS**_
1. <u>Consistent</u> response to a…	* Frequency
2. <u>Recurring</u> situation over a…	* Repetition
3. <u>Substantial</u> period of time	* Longevity
4. <u>Recognized</u> by both Parties.	* Mutuality

THE USES OF PAST PRACTICE

1. Clarifying ambiguous language.

2. Implementing general contract language.

3. Modifying apparently ambiguous language:

    a. Even well-established practices will be insufficient in most cases to overcome clear contract language.

    b. Most arbitrators will deny enforcement if either Party has "slept on their rights through their own practices."

    c. An established practice may give definition to contract modifications from grievance settlements or in other agreements entered into after contract ratification.

4. Past Practices are a separate, enforceable, condition of employment.

WHERE PAST PRACTICE CONTROLS

1. Clarity and consistency.

    a. To be a sustainable, binding Past Practice, the course of conduct must be clearly defined.

    b. It must be viewed as the invariable response given to a specific set of conditions. In short, given "X," the Parties have done "Y."

2. Acceptability.

    a. Both Parties must have knowledge of the practice and accept it as the correct and customary way of dealing with the situation.

3. Mutuality.

    a. The practice must be a product of the Parties' joint understanding as a condition of employment.

4. Longevity and Repetition.

    a. There is no absolute standard as to how long a practice must exist or how frequently it must be utilzed for it to be validated.

CONCLUSIONS

1. A valid Past Practice is as much a part of the contract as any other written provision.

2. A clearly established Past Practice over a lengthy period of time may also amend the apparent language of the contract.

PAST PRACTICE QUIZ 34
ALL TRAINEES

1. List the four concepts of an established Past Practice.
   a.
   b.
   c.
   d.

Circle the appropriate answers.

2. Past Practice controls:
   a. When the practice is clear.
   b. When the practice is ambiguous.
   c. When the practice occurred once.
   d. When the practice happens once every five years.

3. Past Practice is important because:
   a. It helps resolve grievance issues.
   b. It helps define the working relationship of the Parties.
   c. The Parties can use it to validate their positions.

4. Words associated with Past Practices:
   a. Long-standing
   b. Mutually endorsed
   c. Inconsistent
   d. Seldom
   e. Clear
   f. Repetitive

+ For True, 0 for False

5. _____ Past Practices are unwritten clauses in the contract.

6. _____ Past Practices are important because of unambiguous contract clauses.

7. _____ It is a wise strategy to gamble on occasion and try to gain through arbitration what was impossible to achieve at the bargaining table.

8. _____ Past Practices are important because of the complex nature of the employment relationship.

9. _____ Most arbitrators will grant enforcement in the event either Party has "slept on their rights through their own practices."

10. _____ A valid practice is considered part of the contract.

PAST PRACTICE QUIZ 34
ANSWERS

1. List the four concepts of an established Past Practice.

    a.   **Consistent**

    b.   **Recurring**

    c.   **Long-standing**

    d.   **Recognized by both Parties**

Circle the appropriate answers.

2. Past Practice controls:

    a.   **When the practice is clear.**

    b.   When the practice is ambiguous.

    c.   When the practice occurred once.

    d.   When the practice happens once every five years.

3. Past Practice is important because:

    a.   **It helps resolve grievance issues.**

    b.   **It helps define the working relationship of the Parties.**

    c.   **The Parties can use it to validate their positions.**

4. Words associated with Past Practices:

    a.   **Long-standing**   d.   Seldom

    b.   **Mutually endorsed**   e.   **Clear**

    c.   Inconsistent   f.   **Repetitive**

+ For True, 0 for False

5.   **+** Past Practices are unwritten clauses in the contract.

6.   **0** Past Practices are important because of unambiguous contract clauses.

7.   **0** It is a wise strategy to gamble on occasion and try to gain through arbitration what was impossible to achieve at the bargaining table.

8.   **+** Past Practices are important because of the complex nature of the employment relationship.

9.   **0** Most arbitrators will grant enforcement in the event either Party has "slept on their rights through their own practices."

10. **+** A valid practice is considered part of the contract.

EVALUATION

The most significant training information I learned was…	*The best concepts in this training were…*
I wish this part/section _____ could have been done differently by…	*A message to the presenters about making positive changes…*

Generic
The Accused

Role Play

Management Team Packet

MANAGEMENT		ASSOCIATION
Caucus Rooms		**Caucus Space Location........**
Group #1	<u>Joint Meeting Room</u>	<u>Table 1</u>
Group #2	<u>Joint Meeting Room</u>	<u>Table 2</u>
Group #3	<u>Joint Meeting Room</u>	<u>Table 3</u>
Group #4	<u>Joint Meeting Room</u>	<u>Table 4</u>
Group #5	<u>Joint Meeting Room</u>	<u>Table 5</u>

MANAGEMENT

Caucus Rooms

ASSOCIATION

Caucus Space Location........

INSTRUCTIONS #1

1.   Divide into one Management team consisting of two or three trainees.

2.   Divide into one Association team consisting of two or three trainees.

3.   Pick up role-play materials.

4.   The caucus rooms are available:

      A.   Management teams are located:

           1.
           2.
           3.
           4.
           5.

      B.   Association teams are located:

           1.
           2.
           3.
           4.
           5.

5. One designated person from each team will decide where to meet when the Parties are ready to discuss the case.

INSTRUCTIONS #2

1.   Review the scenario.

2.   Management Team:

> Fran Dean
> Val Hammer
> Gerrie Attorney

3.   Association Team:

> Jo Hartford
> Sam Gates
> Lynn Advocate

4.   Devise a meeting strategy in terms of goals and objectives.

5.   Devise a questioning strategy in order to achieve goals and objectives.

6.   _____ minutes to prepare.

7.   _____ minutes for the case.

8.   _____ minutes to debrief.

SCENARIO EXERCISE
THE ACCUSED

Scenario

Jo Hartford was a highly successful seventeen-year employee in the Computer Research Department with a reputation as an outstanding worker at Bend Computer Company. At the beginning of her work career with another company, she was fired because of problems with a young supervisor, Fran Dean. Hartford eventually left the company because of the strained relationship. She believed Dean was out to get her. Jo is currently a member of the Association bargaining team.

Three years ago, Dean was hired as a supervisor of Bend Computer Company. The relationship problems between Hartford and Dean started immediately with ongoing arguments. Their styles were totally different and they clashed constantly.

Jo's significant other, Sam Gates, has been employed as a head computer technician responsible for the computer lab the last ten years. He has been a long-time loyal employee of the company and a past president of the Association. Sam had several confrontations with his supervisor, Val Hammer, when he was Association President. It was "hammer and tong" when they tried to have a conversation to resolve problems. Gates had a history of complaining to Hammer about the lack of maintenance funds and equipment to run a modern-day computer lab.

There were five new computers stored in the back of the computer room that were ordered for the research department to use the next month when a new lab was going to be operational. Dean inventoried the equipment and discovered two computers missing. Dean and Hammer went to the company president and said they observed Hartford and Gates going in and out of the area, both early and late in the evening, acting suspicious on several different occasions. Dean and Hammer made allegations they believed Hartford and Gates had stolen the equipment. They called them to a meeting and accused them of stealing the two computers and demanded the stolen equipment be returned immediately.

CONTRACT PROVISIONS
THE ACCUSED

Relevant Contract Provisions

Article 6 – Grievance Procedure

Section A 1. "Grievance" is defined as a complaint that this Agreement has been violated.

"Employee Grievance" is defined as a complaint by one (1) or more unit members that Management has violated provisions of this Agreement, provided the conduct complained of directly affects the unit member(s).

Section B 1. Representation. A unit member who initiates a grievance may elect to be represented by the Association or the unit member may elect to represent himself/herself at Levels I and II.

Article 9 – Just Cause Section of Contract

A.   No unit member shall be disciplined, reprimanded or reduced in compensation without Just Cause. Reprimands shall be made privately.

E.   Whenever a unit member is directed to meet with a supervisor or other representative of the company regarding a matter which could result in disciplinary action or termination, the unit member shall be given prior written notice of the reasons for such meeting and the right to have either a representative of the Association or legal counsel present to advise the unit member during the meeting.

ROLE PLAY
MANAGEMENT

1. Caucus and prepare case.

2. Management is the moving Party and will start the meeting with the charges.

3. Management wants to suspend Hartford and Gates for five days without pay. (Just Cause.)

4. Also, they want to place a letter of reprimand in each personnel file. (Just Cause.)

5. Make the Association demonstrate and prove all contractual rights.

6. If they ask the right questions, answer them truthfully.

7. Do not make up new facts—instead, stay with the facts in this case.

8. Prepare an opening statement.

9. "Keep it simple" (KISS) approach.

FRAN DEAN & VAL HAMMER
FACT SHEET

1. The Parties have had problems with their working relationship for a long time.

2. Dean is relying heavily on Hammer's words about the missing computers.

3. Hammer is sure Hartford and Gates stole the computers because he has observed them "hanging out" at the computer lab looking suspicious late at night on several different occasions. Consequently, they were the only ones with access to the computers who could have stolen the equipment; no other employees were observed in the area.

4. Dean and Hammer do not feel comfortable around Hartford and Gates.

5. Dean believes Hammer is telling the truth.

6. Challenge the Association's right to representation.

7. Dean and Hammer truly believe Hartford and Gates are guilty.

8. The conflicting Parties have history. Hartford and Gates are gun-control advocates, while Dean and Hammer are gun-toting Western types who drive pickups and like to tree bears with their hound dogs on weekends. Both Parties engaged in heated arguments in the past about gun issues.

EVALUATION

The most significant thing I learned was...	The best things about this workshop were...
I wish...	**A message to the presenters...**

Generic
The Accused

Role Play

Association Team Packet

MANAGEMENT		ASSOCIATION
Caucus Rooms		**Caucus Space Location........**
Group #1	Joint Meeting Room	Table 1
Group #2	Joint Meeting Room	Table 2
Group #3	Joint Meeting Room	Table 3
Group #4	Joint Meeting Room	Table 4
Group #5	Joint Meeting Room	Table 5

MANAGEMENT

Caucus Rooms

ASSOCIATION

Caucus Space
Location........

111

INSTRUCTIONS #1

1. Divide into one Management team consisting of two or three trainees.

2. Divide into one Association team consisting of two or three trainees.

3. Pick up role-play materials.

4. The caucus rooms are available:

    A. Management teams are located:

        1.
        2.
        3.
        4.
        5.

    B. Association Teams are located:

        1.
        2.
        3.
        4.
        5.

5. One designated person from each team will decide where to meet when the Parties are ready to discuss the case.

INSTRUCTIONS #2

1. Review the scenario.

2. Management Team:

    Fran Dean
    Val Hammer
    Gerrie Attorney

3. Association Team:

    Jo Hartford
    Sam Gates
    Lynn Advocate

4. Devise a meeting strategy in terms of goals and objectives.

5. Devise a questioning strategy in order to achieve goals and objectives.

6. _____ minutes to prepare.

7. _____ minutes for the case.

8. _____ minutes to debrief.

SCENARIO EXERCISE
THE ACCUSED

Scenario

Jo Hartford was a highly successful seventeen-year employee in the Computer Research Department with a reputation as an outstanding worker at Bend Computer Company. At the beginning of her work career with another company, she was fired because of problems with a young supervisor, Fran Dean. She eventually left the company because of the strained relationship. Jo believed Dean was out to get her. Hartford is a member of the Association bargaining team.

Three years ago, Dean was hired as a supervisor of Bend Computer Company. The relationship problems between Hartford and Dean started immediately with ongoing arguments. Their styles were totally different and they clashed constantly.

Jo's significant other, Sam Gates, has been employed as a head computer technician responsible for the computer lab the last ten years. He is a long-time loyal employee of the company and a past president of the Association. Sam had several confrontations with his supervisor, Val Hammer when he was Association President. It was "hammer and tong" when they tried to have a conversation to resolve problems. Gates had a history of complaining to Hammer about the lack of maintenance funds and equipment to run a modern day computer lab.

There were five new computers stored in the back of the computer room that were ordered for the research department to use the next month when a new lab was going to be operational. Dean inventoried the equipment and discovered two computers missing. Dean and Hammer went to the company president and said they observed Hartford and Gates going in and out of the area, both early and late in the evening, acting suspicious on several different occasions. Dean and Hammer made allegations they believed Hartford and Gates had stolen the equipment. They called them to a meeting and accused them of stealing the two computers and demanded the stolen equipment be returned immediately.

CONTRACT PROVISIONS
THE ACCUSED

Relevant Contract Provisions

Article 6 – Grievance Procedure

Section A 1. "Grievance" is defined as a complaint that this Agreement has been violated.

"Employee Grievance" is defined as a complaint by one (1) or more unit members that Management has violated provisions of this Agreement, provided the conduct complained of directly affects the unit member(s).

Section B 1. Representation. A unit member who initiates a grievance may elect to be represented by the Association or the unit member may elect to represent himself/herself at Levels I and II.

Article 9 – Just Cause Section of Contract

A.   No unit member shall be disciplined, reprimanded or reduced in compensation without Just Cause. Reprimands shall be made privately.

E.   Whenever a unit member is directed to meet with a supervisor or other representative of the company regarding a matter which could result in disciplinary action or termination, the unit member shall be given prior written notice of the reasons for such meeting and the right to have a representative of the Association or legal counsel present to advise the unit member during the meeting.

ROLE PLAY
ASSOCIATION ADVOCATES

1. Caucus and prepare case.

2. Devise a strategy to help Hartford and Gates.

3. Devise a contract strategy.

    A.   Was the contract violated?
    B.   If so, cite specific examples.
    C.   What are the appropriate remedies?

4. Prepare questions for meeting.

5. Check basic concepts for Just Cause as one basis for questions.

6. Hartford and Gates are totally upset and want to take action now.

7. Do not make up new facts—instead, stay with the facts in this case.

8. Prepare an opening statement.

9. "Keep it simple" (KISS) approach.

JO HARTFORD AND SAM GATES
FACT SHEET

1. There is negative history between the Parties that goes back a long time.

2. Hartford and Gates claim never to have stolen anything. In fact, they are both deacons at their church and are very conservative.

3. They were accused, never questioned, about the allegations.

4. The conflicting Parties have history. Hartford and Gates are gun-control advocates, while Dean and Hammer are gun-toting Western types who drive pickups and like to tree bears with their hound dogs on weekends. The Parties engaged in heated arguments in the past about gun issues.

5. Hartford and Gates have no previous disciplinary actions against them and their evaluations/reviews have been good.

6. Both get along well with all employees.

7. Prior to the accusation, they were not asked to explain their side of the story.

8. Dean and Hammer never provided evidence to support their allegations.

9. There was no prior discussion with them about the theft.

10. Hartford and Gates park their cars behind the computer lab and walk through the lab daily.

11. They often work until late at night since they do not "work the clock." They work many hours beyond the weekly standard in order to get the job done. Also, they are "early birds" who come to work sometimes before other employees.

EVALUATION

The most significant thing I learned was...	The best things about this workshop were...
I wish...	**A message to the presenters...**

OTHER SIMULATIONS

Other simulations for Higher Education, Community College, K–12, both educators and classified, are available from the author at docdengenis@gmail.com or 503.803.4229.

EPILOGUE
ADVOCACY LOST AND FOUND

Advocacy, at times, gets lost in the survival struggle among workers in these dire economic times. Advocacy training of all new leaders is crucial when developing advocate organizations and nurturing new leadership. All people in leadership positions and/or on Association committees or teams should be trained in advocacy. If member leaders do not understand basic advocacy concepts, organizational decisions will not be based on advocacy principles and will be lost in the Association decision-making process.

Contact Information:

Doc Dengenis

Bargaining Consultant

docdengenis@gmail.com

3630 6Th Ave

Suite 301

San Diego, California

92103

503.803.4229

www.ingramcontent.com/pod-product-compliance
Lightning Source LLC
Chambersburg PA
CBHW062028210326
41519CB00060B/7197